Meteor

CHERRY LAKE PRESS

Published in the United States of America by Cherry Lake Publishing
Ann Arbor, Michigan
www.cherrylakepublishing.com

Reading Adviser: Beth Walker Gambro, MS, Ed., Reading Consultant, Yorkville, IL
Book Design: Jennifer Wahi
Illustrator: Jeff Bane

Photo Credits: © Triff/Shutterstock.com, 5, 17; © Belish/Shutterstock.com, 7; © Nazarii_Neshcherenskyi/
Shutterstock.com, 9; © Vadim Sadovski/Shutterstock.com, 11, 15, 19; © Geermy/Shutterstock.com, 13; ©
Zakharchuk/Shutterstock.com, 21; © MARHARYTA MARKO/iStock.com, 23; Cover, 2-3, 6, 12, 22, 24, Jeff Bane

Cherry Lake Press is an imprint of Cherry Lake Publishing Group.

Library of Congress Cataloging-in-Publication Data

Names: Devera, Czeena, author. | Bane, Jeff, 1957- illustrator.
Title: Meteor / by Czeena Devera ; illustrated by Jeff Bane.
Description: Ann Arbor, Michigan : Cherry Lake Publishing, [2022] | Series:
  My guide to the solar system | Includes index. | Audience: Grades K-1 |
Identifiers: LCCN 2021036563 (print) | LCCN 2021036564 (ebook) | ISBN
  9781534199019 (hardcover) | ISBN 9781668900154 (paperback) | ISBN
  9781668901595 (pdf) | ISBN 9781668905913 (ebook)
Subjects: LCSH: Meteors--Juvenile literature.
Classification: LCC QB741.5 .D48 2023 (print) | LCC QB741.5 (ebook) | DDC
  523.5/1--dc23
LC record available at https://lccn.loc.gov/2021036563
LC ebook record available at https://lccn.loc.gov/2021036564

Printed in the United States of America
Corporate Graphics

About the author: Czeena Devera grew up in the red-hot heat of Arizona surrounded by books. Her childhood bedroom had built-in bookshelves that were always full. She now lives in Michigan with an even bigger library of books.

About the illustrator: Jeff Bane and his two business partners own a studio along the American River in Folsom, California, home of the 1849 Gold Rush. When Jeff's not sketching or illustrating for clients, he's either swimming or kayaking in the river to relax.

I'm a **meteor**. You see me in the sky when I enter Earth's **atmosphere**.

People call me a "shooting star." But I'm not a star! I'm just a flash of light you see on Earth.

I'm called a **meteoroid** when I live in space. I'm like a floating rock.

I usually turn into dust when I enter a planet's atmosphere. But if I survive the trip, I'm called a **meteorite**!

What do you think meteor showers look like?

A lot of us enter Earth every day. When there are many of us, it's called a meteor shower.

We come in different sizes.
Most of us are the size of
a pebble.

But we can also be very large.
One of us was so large that it
destroyed the dinosaurs!

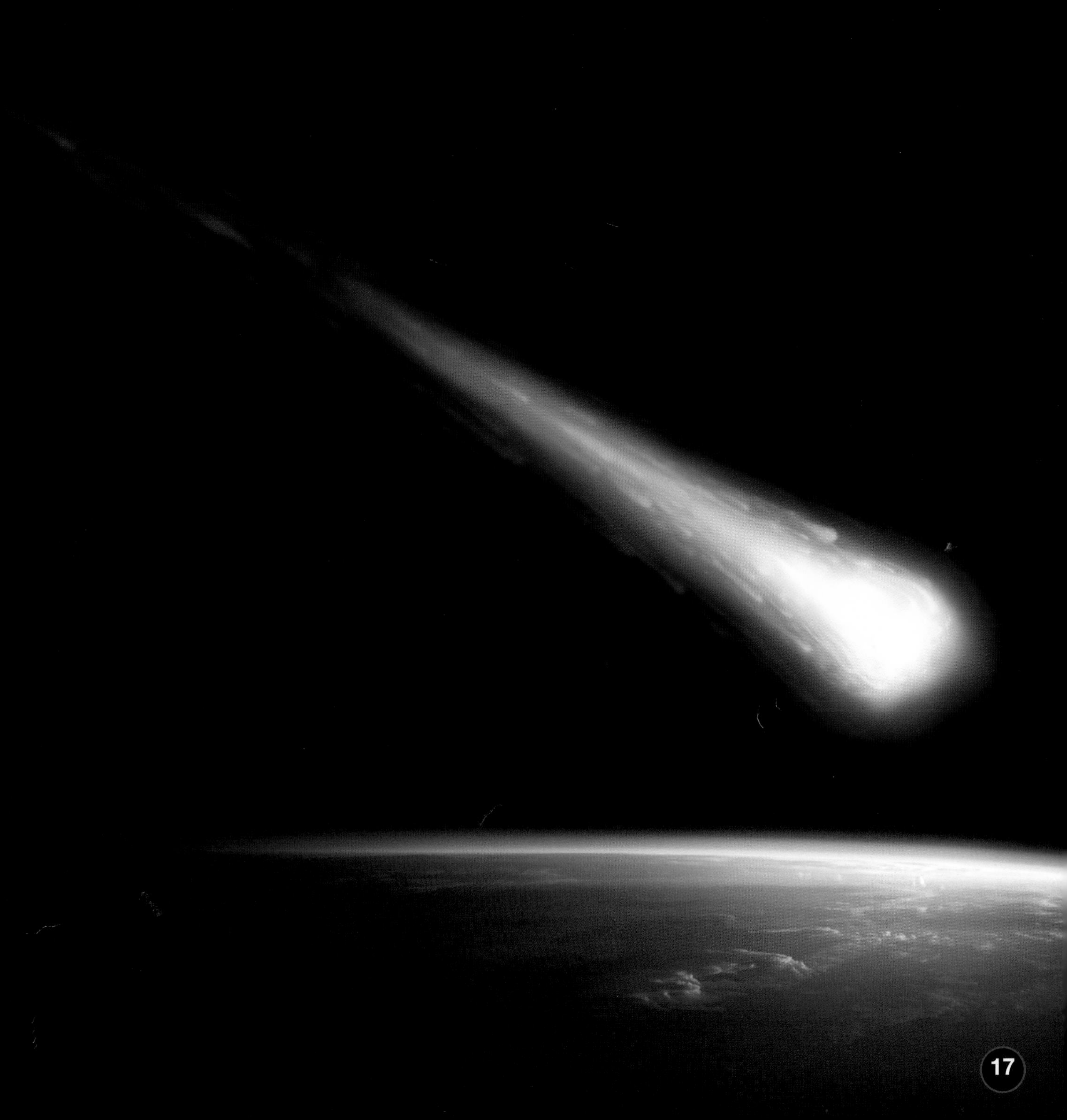

Most of us are broken-off pieces of **asteroids**. But some of us come from planets.

We're pretty old. A lot of us are about 4.6 billion years old. That's how old the **solar system** is.

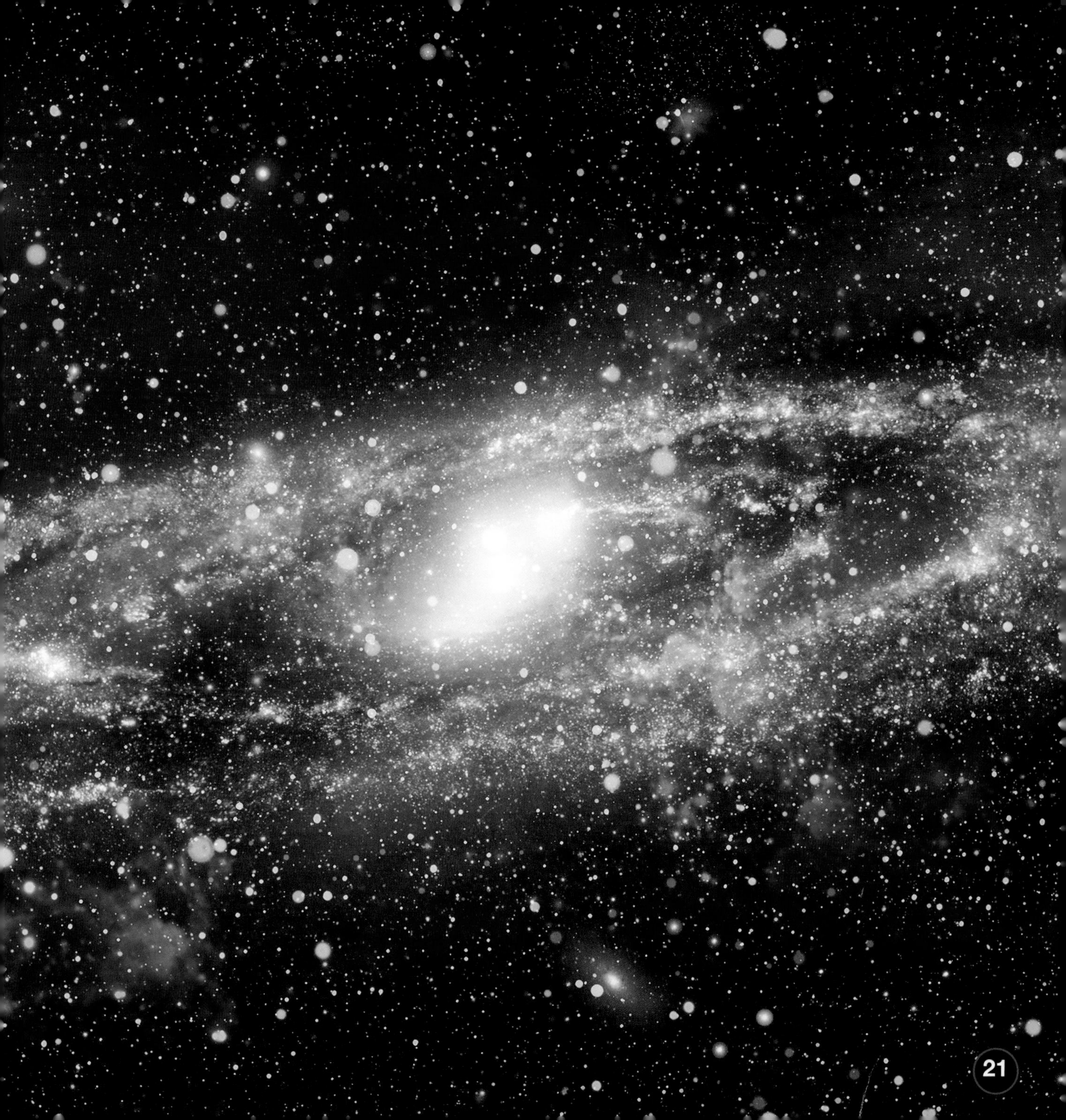

Scientists are still studying me. There's so much more to learn!

glossary

asteroids (A-stuh-roydz) thousands of rocky objects that move in orbits mostly between the planets Mars and Jupiter

atmosphere (AT-MUH-sfeer) the mass of air surrounding a planet or other object in space

meteor (MEE-tee-er) a light phenomenon that results when a meteoroid enters Earth's atmosphere and vaporizes

meteorite (MEE-tee-uh-rahyt) a meteoroid that survives its passage through Earth's atmosphere and lands on Earth's surface.

meteoroid (MEE-tee-uh-roid) a small particle from a comet or asteroid orbiting the sun

scientists (SYE-uhn-tists) people who study nature and the world we live in

solar system (SOH-luhr SIH-stuhm) a star and the planets that move around it

index